Pit Pass

Behind the Scenes of NASCAR

by Bob Woods

Pleasantville, New York • Montréal, Québec • Bath, United Kingdom

Published by Reader's Digest Children's Books
Reader's Digest Road, Pleasantville, NY U.S.A. 10570-7000
and Reader's Digest Children's Publishing Limited,
The Ice House, 124-126 Walcot Street, Bath UK BA1 5BG

10 9 8 7 6 5 4 3 2 1

Manuscript and consulting services provided by
Shoreline Publishing Group LLC.

Library of Congress Cataloging-in-Publication Data

Woods, Bob.
Pit pass : behind the scenes of NASCAR / written by Bob Woods.
p. cm
ISBN 0-7944-0601-7
1. Stock car racing—United States—Juvenile literature. 2. Pit crews—United States—Juvenile literature. 3. NASCAR (Association)—Juvenile literature
I. Title.

GV1029.9.S74W68 2005 796.72—dc22 2004053180

Contents

Introduction:

NASCAR: Inside and Out

"Gentlemen, start your engines!"

That's the official command given to drivers shortly before the green flag drops to start another memorable NASCAR race. Moments later, the track comes alive with the thunderous, high-speed, thrilling action that makes the National Association for Stock Car Auto Racing America's most awesome action sport.

However, the three-plus hours of racing excitement that follow each green flag aren't the whole story of NASCAR. The superstar drivers are in the spotlight, but much less is known about their crew chiefs, mechanics, engineers, designers, and others on their racing team. Racing fans marvel at the multi-colored parade of cars that blaze around the track at speeds up to 200 miles per hour (mph), but do they stop to think about everything that went into actually building each one of those land rockets? Or what it takes to get them ready for a race and keep them going for as many as 600 grueling miles?

The scene at Daytona, Bristol, Darlington, Talladega, and some of the other historic racetracks on those glorious Sunday afternoons is incredible, but what's happening there during the rest of the week? Millions of viewers love watching NASCAR races on TV, because the broadcasters do such a great job of showing and explaining what's going on. What the folks at home don't see, though, are the people who operate dozens of TV cameras, or the researchers who gather mounds of information for the announcers, or the truck drivers who haul tons of equipment from race to race.

NASCAR Pit Pass tells the entire story of a NASCAR NEXTEL Cup Series race, from building the team to building the car engine, from prerace inspections in the garage area to postrace celebrations in Victory Lane. What does a team owner do? What's the big deal about ace driver Ryan Newman having a college degree? What makes one track different from another? What goes on in the broadcast booth during the race? You'll learn the answers to these questions and many more in this book.

You'll also learn how race teams assemble a race

car's roll cage, chassis (pronounced "CHASS-ee"), and suspension. You can check out the inside of a car, as seen from the driver's point of view. Go behind the scenes in the garage area. Meet the TV producer for NBC-TV's NASCAR coverage. Experience a pit stop, second by second.

The very first "strictly stock" NASCAR race was run in 1949 on a three-quarter-mile dirt track at Charlotte Speedway in North Carolina. Nearly 13,000 curious fans showed up to watch 33 drivers battle it out for 150 miles. (Most drove their family cars rather than a specially designed race car.) The race was a good one (even though the winner was disqualified for cheating), but pretty simple compared to today's extravaganzas. Think of the Wright Brothers' first airplane flight vs. a space shuttle blastoff. Humble as it was, that first race was extremely important. It marked the beginning of a sport that has changed and grown into a national phenomenon. Today, NASCAR—along with its drivers, crews, officials, track workers, and fans—has become part of our culture.

So if you're ready: Readers, start your engines, turn your pages, and discover what the exciting world of NASCAR is all about!

At some NASCAR tracks, the turns are steeply angled, or "banked." Banking allows cars to keep their speed up in the curves.

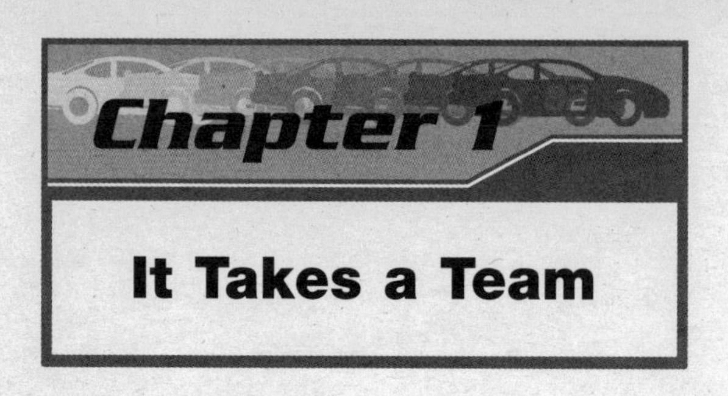

Chapter 1

It Takes a Team

Dale Earnhardt Jr. roared under the checkered flag in his No. 8 Chevy at the thrilling conclusion of the 2004 Daytona 500. Moments later, he summed up what it takes to win a NASCAR race. “There’s a lot of work done behind the scenes by guys who never get the credit,” he said, interrupting the post-race celebration so he could thank those guys. Sure, Dale Jr. was the famous star buckled in behind the wheel for more than three hours that afternoon. Yes, he was the one battling 42 of the world’s best stock car drivers for 200 laps at an average speed over 150 mph. But he knew that his narrow victory—“Little E’s” first-ever in the Great American Race—wouldn’t have been possible without the combined efforts of a multi-talented team of individual experts.

NASCAR is the ultimate team sport. Fans watching races at the track or on TV at home cheer for their favorite drivers and the awesome cars they pilot. It’s not like football, basketball, hockey, or baseball, where fans root, root, root for the home team of players out there together. The teammates of Dale Earnhardt, Kurt Busch, Jeff Gordon, Jimmie Johnson, Matt Kenseth, Ryan Newman, and other top NASCAR drivers do their special things mostly out of sight. The notable exceptions are the mad-dashing pit crews that grab about 20 seconds of spotlight time with every frenzied stop for tires, gas, and a cold drink. Yet few fans know their names—even though any one of them can make the difference between winning and finishing anywhere else in the pack.

You can be sure the drivers know who they are, along with the dozens of other unsung heroes who make up a NASCAR team. When you stop to think about what each person does to get the car and driver out on the track—and keep them going 'round week after week—you can appreciate the crucial role that teamwork plays in auto racing. From the team owner to the crew chief, from mechanics to truck drivers, they comprise the well-oiled machines that make NASCAR run so well.

The situation was much simpler back in the 1930s and 1940s when stock car racing was getting up and running on oval dirt tracks throughout the Carolinas,

Georgia, and other Southern states. If a driver wanted to race, he would simply show up at the track with his car, pay a nominal entry fee, and "get after it."

Legendary pioneers such as Ralph Earnhardt (the late Dale Earnhardt's father and Dale Jr.'s grandfather), Lee Petty, Red Byron, and Junior Johnson were pretty much one-man shows. They owned their "rides"—lingo for race cars—set them up for competition, and did every stitch of work on the engines. The fortunate ones may have had a mechanically minded brother, cousin, or friend who could help out and lend a hand in the pits.

By the time Bill France organized the rapidly growing sport by forming NASCAR in 1948, the team concept was gradually emerging. Bigger and faster tracks were springing up across the country, attracting more and more drivers and their loyal fans. Before long, there was a race held somewhere on the expanding NASCAR circuit almost every weekend. Soon it became nearly impossible for a lone driver to handle the many details by himself. There were also rising costs to keep racing all season. The driver had to pay mechanics and pit crews, maintain more than one car and multiple engines, and travel from track to track.

Drivers received financial help from Ford, Chevy,

Brian Vickers confers with his crew chief
Peter Sospenzo.

Dodge, and the other automakers. Oil and gas companies, tire manufacturers, and other corporations also started sponsoring drivers. But sponsors demanded winning results in exchange for investing their money. NASCAR was becoming a big business, and the little guy on his own couldn't keep pace.

Fast forward to the 21st century, where the NASCAR NEXTEL Cup Series is dominated by huge, sophisticated teams. It costs around $15 million a year to run a car in every NASCAR NEXTEL Cup Series race. While the driver is the most visible member of a team—and most teams have two or three drivers—the owner is the one who keeps the wheels turning. Think of the driver as a quarterback directing the action down the football field, or a point guard calling out plays on the basketball court. That driver or that quarterback would be nowhere without his team's owner. The owner is the one who puts all the other players around the star driver or quarterback. The NASCAR team owner does the hiring and firing of team members. He arranges to buy the cars, engines, tools, and everything else needed to be a part of NASCAR. He or she—Teresa Earnhardt now owns Dale Earnhardt Inc. (DEI)—pays the bills by convincing sponsors the team can win races and

Top 10 All-Time Team Owner Wins

Rank	Team Owner	Wins
1)	Petty Enterprises	271*
2)	Junior Johnson	139
3)	Hendrick Motorsports	126*
4)	Wood Brothers	97*
5)	Holman-Moody	92
6)	Richard Childress Racing	76*
7)	Roush Racing	73*
8)	Bud Moore	63
9)	Robert Yates Racing	56*
9)	Roger Penske	56*
10)	Carl Kiekhaefer	54

*active owner (totals as of September 26, 2004)

championships. In other words, the owner is the boss.

When it comes to the business of having the cars running smoothly before, during, and after a race, the buck stops with the crew chief. He's the team's coach, the guy who keeps all the different crew members working together every day, on and off the track. Because he's responsible for seeing so many jobs get done properly and on time, the crew chief wears many hats. As the coach, he motivates, energizes, and communicates with the troops. He's the lead mechanic, too, making sure various team members maintain the cars in tip-top shape. Those crew members include engine builders, brake specialists, chassis fabricators, transmission technicians, and more. Then, on race day, the crew chief becomes the pit boss. He tells the pit crew exactly what needs to be done during each pit stop.

And there's plenty to be done once the pit crew goes "over the wall" during a race. The jack man instantly jacks up the car. There are two tire changers, one for the front wheels, the other for the rear, plus two tire carriers. The gas man fills the tank. His partner, the gas catch man, handles any fuel that spills. Less than half a minute later, the jack man lowers the car, and off it peels back onto the track. (For a detailed description of "life in the pits," see chapter 6.)

Other members of the team jump into action once the race is over and immediately begin preparing for the next one. If the driver finished in the top three or four places, several mechanics assist in the official postrace "tear-down" where NASCAR officials inspect the car to make sure it meets the rules. Then a crew loads everything, from race cars to screwdrivers, onto a two-level, 18-wheel transporter truck. Before long, the truck driver steers the big rig onto the highway, back to the team's headquarters. Depending on the distance, the rest of the team follows by car or plane. On Monday morning, the process starts all over again.

There's a ton of paperwork and office duties performed by a NASCAR team, too. So teams also need a staff that includes marketing, advertising and public relations experts, accountants, secretaries, and receptionists.

Win or lose, the owner—the boss—appreciates each and every member of the team. "It's always great to be in Victory Lane," Teresa Earnhardt told reporters the day after her stepson won the 2004 Daytona 500. "I'm proud of not only Dale Jr., but of all the people at DEI for working hard."

That Old-time Teamwork

When Benny Parsons began his stock car racing career in the early 1960s, the typical "team" was pretty simple.

"Me and one guy worked on the car all day," recalls Parsons, who is now an analyst for NASCAR coverage on NBC and TNT. "At six that night, three more guys who spent all day at their various jobs would show up, and we worked on the car until 11. And on Friday nights we went racing somewhere.

"Most of those guys were volunteers," says Parsons, who joined NASCAR's Cup Series circuit in 1970. "The teams were not nearly as professional then as they are today, because you spent all your time working on the race car. You didn't have a lot of time to practice pit stops, for instance."

Most drivers had a crew chief, simply because they couldn't make decisions when they were in the race car. "The crew chief also worked on the car," says Parsons. "He was an integral part of getting the car ready to go. Today, the crew chief does very little mechanical work on the car."

Sponsorship was a much different concept as

well. "Most of the sponsors were local businesses, like Bill's Garage or Bob's Gulf, people who gave you very little money." So there wasn't much to go around, even for the simplest of things. "We went to bowling alley stores to get some uniforms," Parsons remembers, "and had someone stitch 'Benny's Racing Team' on the back."

Parson's first NASCAR team was owned by a man who ran a trucking company and a farm in tiny Ellerbe, North Carolina, not far from the famous track in Rockingham. "He had a crew chief/engine builder, and about two other people working on the car." They did quite a job, however, helping Parsons win the NASCAR Cup Series championship in 1973 and the Daytona 500 in 1975. Parsons retired after the 1988 season and ten years later was named one of the "50 Greatest Drivers in NASCAR History."

Chapter 2

Build It and They Will Race

In the wide world of sports, there's nothing quite equal to a NASCAR race car. The look of the car says awesome power, blinding speed, road-hugging handling, and pure muscle. The thunderous sound speaks volumes about pedal-to-the-metal horsepower and high-tech engineering. It's a lean, mean, bold, and beautiful racing machine!

As we marvel at NASCAR's brightly colored land rockets, adorned from bumper to bumper with familiar product logos and other bold graphics, it's easy to take for granted what goes into building one. We don't stop to consider the hours spent by teams of highly trained designers, fabricators, and mechanics creating these handmade, four-wheeled masterpieces. There's Ryan Newman drafting his black-and-white No. 12 Dodge inches behind a rival at 150 mph, then executing a perfect slingshot pass on a banked turn.

Mechanics are key members of any NASCAR team.

Looks great, right? But few fans are thinking about the wind-tunnel tests that helped develop the car's aerodynamics (the science of improving airflow around the car to reduce drag).

Although they're called "stock cars," there's actually very little stock that goes into them anymore. The term originated during the sport's early days in the 1930s, referring to family sedans that really did go from the dealer's showroom floor (the dealer's "stock" of cars) to the racetrack. But because the goal has always been about going faster than the other guy, drivers inevitably started tinkering with their racers. They'd modify the carburetor to boost the horsepower of the engine, install heavier shocks to improve handling on the rugged dirt tracks, or re-gear the transmission to gain a bit more speed.

The bodies of the cars, however, weren't tampered with much then. Whether it was a Ford coupe, Hudson Hornet, Nash Ambassador, Chrysler 300, Dodge Coronet, or other popular "rides" of the day, they didn't look much different from the street models. Some changes they usually made included removing the headlights and side mirrors and painting numbers and driver names on the doors. What was inside the car was what counted, and what separated winners from also-rans.

NASCAR leveled the playing field in the 1950s by outlawing modified cars from its top divisions and declaring that all drivers run "strictly stock" cars. Engines, suspensions, transmissions, brakes, tires, and other standard components had to be the same for everyone. That's also when the first paved superspeedways were constructed, raising not only the speeds of the cars, but the degree of danger, too. So NASCAR began demanding that certain safety equipment be installed. Two of the most important innovations were welded steel side supports and roll bars to prevent injuries in smash-ups and rollovers. Driver helmets, seats, and tires were upgraded, as well. Safety would become a major issue in NASCAR, to the point where today's cars are equipped to ensure that drivers can survive high-speed crashes, flips, and fires.

By the 1960s, the outsides of stock cars started to evolve. Ford, General Motors, Dodge, and other Detroit automakers formed dedicated "motorsports" divisions. They supplied standard bodies and other key parts to specialty racing shops, which altered the original designs—within strict NASCAR guidelines—to produce more and more unique cars. Fenders, hoods, and roofs were sculpted to improve aerodynamics and acceleration. The addition of front air ducts and a rear spoiler (wing-like horizontal metal blade attached to the rear deck lid) aided stability and traction.

The evolution of the stock car is ongoing, with speed, handling, and safety remaining the driving—if sometimes conflicting—forces. A step-by-step look at how a modern car is built showcases the exhilaration, technology, and creativity that combine to make NASCAR America's most thrilling sport.

The process, lasting several months, begins with computers and software that a team uses to "build" the entire car on a screen in 3-D. The design program allows them to input the range of real-world factors, such as airflow, heat, track conditions, and NASCAR-required car height, width, length, and weight. The computer generates a digital blueprint, which will serve as the master plan each step of the way.

Then it's time to move into the garage, with the nuts and bolts, steel and rubber. Much as a skeleton's bones provide the basic framework for a human body, a stock car is built around an intricate steel frame called the chassis. The core structure is the roll cage, a series of thick steel tubes welded together to form a protective box surrounding the driver. Following rigid NASCAR safety rules, it will hold up under extreme pressure during an accident.

From there, other pieces of the chassis are added. Especially crucial is the firewall, a plate of steel separating the driver compartment from the engine, which grows incredibly hot during a race. There's another one between the driver and the trunk, where the 22-gallon fuel cell is located. The floor panel is a sheet of metal that serves as the car's floor. Four semicircular steel fender wells form the spaces for the wheels and tires.

The race car body fits over this super-strong, steel skeleton. Referring to the digital blueprint—and keeping to NASCAR guidelines—team members known as fabricators cut and shape sheet metal to form the hood, roof, fenders, side panels, and other body parts. Ryan Newman's car might technically be a Dodge Intrepid, and Tony Stewart's is a Chevrolet Monte Carlo, but they barely resemble the Intrepids and Monte Carlos seen on the road. And Newman's Intrepid is slightly different from Rusty Wallace's, which is different from Sterling Marlin's.

The various body pieces are securely attached to the chassis, one by one, with nail-like metal rivets. Next, all the pieces are welded together and smoothed to create a seamless metal skin, ready to be painted. Because everything's steel, a coat of rustproof primer is applied

One of Matt Kenseth's cars gets a once-over before the race.

first, followed by the paint and a slew of decals—including ones that appear to be headlights. For safety's sake, there are no real lights, nor windows or doors on a NASCAR car. (The driver climbs in through his window area, which is covered by a protective net.)

The cockpit, or interior, of the car is now ready to be outfitted. There won't be any passengers, so only the driver's seat is needed, including seat belts and other safety gear, along with the gauge-filled dashboard.

One of the most critical parts of a stock car is what's underneath it—the suspension, a system of springs and shock absorbers. Combined with the axles, wheels, tires, and brakes, the suspension determines how a car handles. The distances, curves, and banking vary from track to track, therefore race teams spend hours before each race adjusting the suspension for specific conditions, a process called the setup. Drivers don't want the setup to be too "loose," meaning that it wiggles back and forth in turns, or "tight," meaning that it's difficult to turn. Even during a race, the setup can be changed in the pits to correct these problems.

Building a race car is a long process, but doing it right can produce long-lasting rewards. Keep that in mind the next time your favorite driver—and his trusty stock car—take the checkered flag.

Ryan Newman: Engineer Behind the Wheel

Ryan Newman speaks a different language than most NASCAR drivers, and we're not talking about French or Spanish. Thanks to his college degree in vehicle structure engineering from Purdue University, the 2002 NASCAR Raybestos Rookie of the Year can discuss things in technical terms that would make most people's head spin. That education comes in handy, on and off the track.

"My crew chief, Matt Borland, and others on the team also have engineering degrees, so we have a common language and background to work with in terms of trying to make the race car fast," says Newman, who drives the No. 12 Dodge for Penske Racing *really* fast. "It definitely helps, because we all have a likeness in thinking when we try and set up the car for certain tracks."

Knowing the precise science behind aerodynamics, drafting, and other principles that apply to auto racing

allows Ryan to contribute to the building of the race car, too. He understands how everything works, and is able to share his knowledge, making him a more complete member of the team. "It isn't just the engineering background," Newman explains, "it's also the communication skills so I can be a better teammate. One of the biggest things I learned in college was communication."

Speed vs. Safety

NASCAR drivers face a constant dilemma. They want their cars to go as fast as possible, so they can win races, compete for the championship every season, satisfy fans and sponsors, and earn lots of money. But at the same time, they also want the cars to be as safe as possible.

To create the best speed, teams test a car's aerodynamics in a wind tunnel. By seeing how air flows around the car, they can alter its shape to reduce drag and gain speed. Mechanics can also adjust the suspension to help the car handle better, and go faster, on curves.

In January 2003, NASCAR opened a new Research and Development Center in Concord, North Carolina, primarily as a high-tech safety testing facility. They use computers to simulate different situations involving crashes and accidents. To test seat belts and other restraints, crash-test dummies are employed.

One of the center's big projects is a five-year plan to build a race car of the future, with safety as a prime factor. "We've focused on the driver's space and what protects the driver: restraint systems, the seat, and the

space around him," Gary Nelson, supervisor of the center, told *National Geographic News*. The prototype car they're testing "got a bit bigger," Nelson adds. "It looks the same, but just a few inches, from the driver's perspective, is a big deal."

Vroom with a View

You'd think a car that costs $15 million a year to operate would at least have a CD player in it. Sorry, but the only music a NASCAR driver might hear inside the cockpit of his car is the whistling of the wind as he roars around the racetrack.

Life inside a stock car is all business, without a whole lot of comfort. Besides having no tunes, there's no air-conditioning, heat, or even extra padding in the driver's seat. There are cooling fans and a radio…but only for communicating with the pit crew and spotters. (Spotters are team members who sit high up at the track and relay a bird's-eye view of the race to the driver.)

It may not be cushy, but the cockpit is an incredibly safe environment. The seat, which is bolted directly to the roll cage, is designed to wrap tightly to the driver's ribs and shoulders. He's further held in by

Dashboards are simple and stripped-down in NASCAR race cars.

a five-part seat belt: two straps secure his shoulders; two wrap around his waist; one fits between his legs. Finally, a special head-and-neck restraint protects the driver from injuries above the shoulders.

NASCAR drivers are required to wear a safety helmet and visor. They can choose between a full-face helmet, which covers everything from the neck up, or an open-face model, which doesn't come across the mouth and chin. Underneath the hard, glossy outer shell is a shock-absorbing foam layer. A third layer is made of fireproof material.

Drivers must wear a heat-resistant suit, gloves, socks, and shoes, too. They provide a safeguard in case a fire breaks out.

Safe and snug in his seat, wearing his helmet (complete with a cooling system) and suit, the driver views the track ahead of him through a windshield made of a thick, shatterproof plastic called Lexan. The rear windshield is made from the same material. The driver sees behind him using a small, round side mirror and a long, horizontal mirror mounted at the top of the inside of the windshield.

The driver also watches a variety of switches and three gauges on the dashboard. The switches control the starter, ignition, and cooling fans. The kill switch shuts off the engine in an emergency. The tachometer is a gauge that measures the RPMs (revolutions per minute) of the engine to show how hard it's working. These cars don't have speedometers. Instead, drivers use RPMs to measure their speed. Separate gauges give readings on the engine's oil and water temperature. Others measure the electrical system and pressure in the fuel cell.

While the cockpit is where the driver does his work—call it the brains of the business—the heart of the operation beats under the hood: the engine. It's a powerful combination of stationary and moving parts, built to precise specifications and finely tuned to run at peak efficiency.

Teams either build their own engines or buy them from outside engine makers. These eight-cylinder race-car engines are considerably larger than typical car engines. Each cylinder contains a piston, which moves up and down rapidly. The pistons generate enormous "horsepower." One horsepower is what it takes to lift 550 pounds one foot high in one second. The engine of a passenger car on the street kicks out about 200 horsepower. A stock car engine produces up to 750 horsepower! NASCAR rules state that every car's horsepower be about the same.

An adequate supply of racing tires is a must for a NASCAR racing team.

As in most cars, these have internal-combustion engines. Inside each cylinder, a mixture of air and gasoline is ignited by a spark plug to cause a series of mini-explosions, that create the power to move the pistons. The pistons are connected to the crankshaft. The crankshaft rotates the crank, a shaft that connects to the transmission.

The engine powers the car's four-speed, manual transmission. The transmission consists of four gears that connect to the front and rear axles, which turn the wheels. Manual means the driver has to shift gears by using the clutch. (Most passenger cars today have transmissions that shift gears automatically.)

In the past, teams travelled to a race with up to seven engines for each car. One was used to qualify for the driver's pole position, or place on the starting grid. (The driver with the fastest qualifying time starts at the best spot—the inside front spot on the first row on the grid.) Another engine was for practice. The rest were for the race itself—with spares in case something went wrong and an engine blew. Today, however, NASCAR has a rule stating a team can only use one engine per weekend.

An engine's greatest enemy is heat, which gets intense when running all out for several hours. So keeping the engine cool—using oil, water, and air—is a major concern. The oil inside the engine lubricates the many moving parts and protects against excessive wear and friction, which can build up heat. Water and chemical coolants are pumped into the engine, too, through a system of heavy-duty hoses and the radiator. The radiator is a squarish device attached to the front of the engine. Cool air passes through the car's front grill openings to the radiator.

With the stock car's chassis, body, engine, and transmission set to go, and the driver suited up and strapped inside the cockpit, the race car is ready to roll. This is where the rubber meets the road, as the saying goes, on a set of four racing tires. They may have a familiar manufacturer's name on the sidewalls, but these are quite different from the tires on your family's car.

For one thing, they don't have any treads. Racing tires are made from a rubbery compound that heats up once the car is barreling around the track at high speeds. The heated compound becomes sticky, helping the tires grip the track surface better. Having treads would mean less rubber on the road.

The track surface, curves, and banking vary from track to track. So, for example, the tires wear down differently at Daytona, a long track, than at Bristol, a short one. Therefore, different compounds are used to make the tires depending on where the race is held. Of course, changing worn tires is one of the main reasons for making a pit stop (see chapter 6).

Don't think the tire changers are filling the tires with air. Most often it's compressed nitrogen, which contains less moisture than compressed air. As the tires heat up, moisture inside causes them to expand and the pressure to increase. Tire pressure affects the car's setup during a race, so using nitrogen gives the race team more control.

Actually, it's a good thing there isn't a CD player in a stock car. With everything that a driver and his team have to deal with, changing discs probably wouldn't be a top priority.

Getting on Track

Labor Day had always been a quaint, all-American holiday in the small town of Darlington, South Carolina. The finale of the traditional three-day, end-of-summer weekend was filled with family picnics, barbecues, and, of course, the annual Labor Day parade. That all changed on the afternoon of September 4, 1950, when NASCAR roared into Darlington.

Just two years old, NASCAR—"Big Bill" France's stock car association—was still building a name for itself on the national sports scene. It had some great personalities in drivers such as Buck Baker, the Flock brothers Tim and Fonty, Lee Petty, Marshall Teague, and Glenn "Fireball" Roberts. And their "rides"—strictly stock Fords, Chevys, Dodges, and the like—dazzled growing crowds of fans at the tracks where they zoomed 'round and 'round. They were dirt tracks, though, and while those dusty ovals held local charm

A race official waves the yellow caution flag.

as the birthplaces of stock car racing, they lacked the grandeur of New York's Yankee Stadium or Chicago's Soldier Field.

Harold Brasington's little hometown sat far from New York or Chicago, but that didn't keep the Darlington businessman from dreaming a big-city dream. His friends had laughed when he returned from the 1933 Indianapolis 500, and suggested that their tiny town could be the home of a superspeedway to rival the Hoosier State's famed Indianapolis Motor Speedway. Brasington was undeterred by his friends' reactions. It took the determined Brasington 16 years to make his dream come true. But in 1949, when the bulldozers started excavating 70 acres of former cotton fields, all the snickering stopped. A year later, NASCAR had its very first paved track, and the inaugural Southern 500 launched a brand-new Labor Day tradition in Darlington.

In that first race at Darlington, a crowd of 25,000 fans cheered on Californian Johnny Mantz as he sped to a victory in that debut 500-miler. In the more than half a century since that race, Darlington Raceway has become one of NASCAR's most hallowed, and challenging, tracks. In addition to the Southern 500, the unique 1.36-mile (originally 1.25 miles), egg-shaped oval hosts the NASCAR NEXTEL Cup Series Carolina Dodge Dealers 400 every March, plus several other major NASCAR events. A Who's Who of great drivers has wheeled into Darlington's Victory Lane—legendary names like David Pearson, Cale Yarborough, Richard Petty, Dale Earnhardt, and Jeff Gordon—but the facility has attained superstardom in its own right.

Indeed, every one of the 32 tracks on NASCAR's premier NASCAR NEXTEL Cup Series possesses a distinct personality and history. Darlington, for example, was intentionally designed so the third and fourth turns were narrow and tricky. The quirky reason why is even part of NASCAR lore. The man from whom Brasington bought the land, Sherman Ramsey, insisted in the deal that a minnow pond on the property remain untouched. The result is a challenging and tricky track that's given rise to a unique term called "the Darlington stripe." The "stripe" gets its name from all the marks left by cars that have scraped against the track walls. It's no wonder that Darlington—the granddaddy of superspeedways—is known as the track that's "too tough to tame." The late Dale Earnhardt, who tamed it nine times, once said, "If you happen to be a race car driver, there's no victory so sweet, so memorable, as whipping Darlington Raceway."

Bristol Motor Speedway is remarkable for its high-banked, half-mile track, producing stock car racing's equivalent of roller derby. At the much-longer tracks at Daytona and Talladega (2.5 miles and 2.66 miles long, respectively), speed restrictions lead to pack racing and drafting. The twisty-turny road courses at Watkins Glen and Infineon (formerly Sears Point) require far more braking, turning, and shifting than on typical ovals.

Shapes and conditions may vary from track to track. However, today's modern venues also feature standard areas and services. Some are what would be expected at most outdoor sports facilities: spacious parking lots; concession stands serving a variety of food and beverages; ticket booths; souvenir shops selling all types of memorabilia; and plenty of grandstand seating. Then there are the behind-the-scenes places specific to NASCAR, where racing teams and officials do their thing.

Other than the actual paved track, perhaps the busiest spot is the garage area, where members of every race team create a buzzing hive of activity throughout a race weekend. However, the prerace preparations begin days before. Earlier in the week, at their team headquarters, mechanics and engineers have slaved over as many as five cars, setting up the engines, chassis, and suspensions for that particular track. Then the cars were loaded onto haulers, along with tons of other necessary gear, and delivered to the track. Bright and early Friday morning at 5 A.M., these 18-wheel trucks are at the track and being unloaded. The teams are raring and ready to go.

The garage area is a gigantic, wide-open space that sits behind pit road. Each team is assigned its own section, where they arrange everything from toolboxes to lounge chairs. For the next three days, this will be home-away-from-home—as well as shop-away-from-shop—for the busy crews. Before fine-tuning the cars for the day's practice and qualifying runs, there's some official business to be done. By 7 A.M. Friday, the cars are expected to be ready for the first of several NASCAR inspections that are conducted during the weekend. Dozens of inspectors check over just about every inch of every car, inside and out, to be sure they adhere to strict safety and competition standards. (Read the accompanying story on page 47 for more details on the inspection process.)

In the past, NASCAR would allow a limited number of visitors to tour the garage area at certain times during race weekends. These lucky fans could get an up-close glimpse at the cars and a chance to meet the drivers and ask for autographs. But with the sport's soaring popularity, it became impossible to accommodate all the fans who wanted to see the garage areas without interfering with the teams' duties. Today, garage passes are reserved to team members and their authorized guests.

Still NASCAR remains one of the most fan-friendly sports, and fans still have many opportunities to see their favorite drivers. "Our athletes are the most accessible in the world, and we want to keep it that way," Jim Hunter, NASCAR's vice president of corporate communications, told the *St. Petersburg Times* in 2002. "We want to look at how we manage security in the garage area and around the haulers, and where fans do have access in our sport and don't have access in other sports."

Nonetheless, at some tracks, fans can purchase prerace passes with access to pit road. They can get a feel for the frenzy that takes place when the seven-person pit crews go "over the wall" to perform their split-second maintenance routines during a race.

For those NASCAR fans who can't make it to the track, the media corps covering the races more than takes up the slack. Dozens of television, radio, newspaper, magazine, and web-site reporters, writers, and broadcasters fill up the press area, which stretches along the top of the grandstands. Armed with laptop computers, telephones, cameras, microphones, and other tools of the journalism trade, the media have a bird's-eye view of the action and relay it to millions of viewers, listeners, and readers. This press section is their permanent perch, but roving reporters also spread out around the track, in the garages, pits, grandstands, and other key vantage points. (For a closer look at how the media cover NASCAR, read chapter 5.)

As NASCAR continues to evolve into America's most popular spectator sport, the tracks, too, are undergoing constant changes and improvements. Much is being done to make the fans more comfortable and involved, including upgraded infield areas, concessions, and grandstands. At the same time, increasing the drivers' safety remains a never-ending goal.

One of the most important programs is the ongoing installation of SAFER (Steel and Foam Energy-Reducing) barriers at more and more tracks. They are designed to replace the concrete outside retaining walls and provide a better way to protect cars that go out of control. The SAFER system, developed by researchers at the Midwest Roadside Safety Facility at the

University of Nebraska-Lincoln, is basically a high-tech shock absorber that reduces the impact to the driver during a crash. "Our goal is to have the SAFER barrier up at every track where it's recommended by the experts by 2005," says Gary Nelson, NASCAR's managing director of research and development.

One of the first tracks to install the SAFER walls was none other than historic Darlington Raceway. Unfortunately, a few months earlier, NASCAR announced that its annual Labor Day race would be shifted to California Speedway outside of Los Angeles. (Darlington will still host the Southern 500, now scheduled for November.) So while the town's end-of-summer weekend will change yet again, its fabled track, while safer, might still be "too tough to tame."

Gadget Inspectors

As the saying goes, "cheaters never prosper"...but they'll also never stop trying to buck the odds. Faced with that unfortunate element of human nature, the NASCAR NEXTEL Cup Series director dispatches about 50 inspectors to race sites every weekend to ensure that its strict rules are enforced.

Since NASCAR's beginnings, drivers and their mechanics have tried rigging their cars to gain an advantage. In fact, in its very first strictly stock event, a 150-mile race on June 19, 1949, at Charlotte Speedway in North Carolina, an unscrupulous scheme was foiled. When the dust settled at the dirt track, it appeared Glenn Dunnaway had won the day. However, when postrace inspectors discovered modified springs supporting the rear of his '47 Ford, Dunnaway was disqualified and Jim Roper was declared the victor.

Today's drivers must submit their cars to at least three inspections during a race weekend. Beginning on Friday morning, before anyone hits the track, the points leader goes first, then everyone else in order of current standings. Inspectors will end up checking each car's body, safety features, chassis, engine, fuel

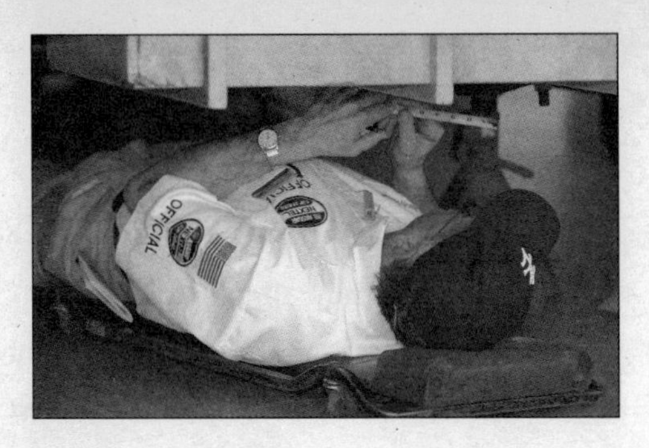

cell, height, and weight.

They use 32 different templates—precise metal cutouts that fit over key areas of the car—to make sure measurements meet NASCAR rules. Cars are rolled onto scales to check the minimum weight: 3,400 pounds, minus the driver. A special stick verifies the correct height. The initial inspection can last from four to ten hours. A shorter inspection is conducted before qualifying and the race. There are also inspections after qualifying runs. Following the race, the top five finishers and others chosen randomly are put through a final checkup, including a complete teardown of the engine.

If an illegal part is found, it can be put on view for other teams to see. In some instances, the entire car is impounded, leaving the guilty team to race a backup. In any case, the rule-breakers can be fined.

For play purposes only.

№ 0001

NAME

This pass is not transferable.

NOT GOOD FOR GRANDSTAND SEATING

Ricky Craven's Chevrolet Monte Carlo gets a last-minute inspection.

Tony Stewart checks the earpiece of his communications system.

NASCAR fan Dwayne Johnson—"The Rock"

NASCAR officials use special, colored metal templates to make sure each race car is the right size and shape.

Bobby Labonte's pit crew

NASCAR drivers Johnny Sauter and Robby Gordon share a lighter moment during a race weekend.

Fender benders are an occasional hazard for NASCAR drivers.

NASCAR fans watch as teams unload their cars and gear.

They've Got NASCAR Covered

Television viewers who tuned into ABC's *Wide World of Sports* on February 15, 1976, received a nice surprise. They were expecting to see events from the Winter Olympic Games in Innsbruck, Austria. Instead, viewers were whisked live to Daytona International Speedway for the grand finale of NASCAR's season-opening Daytona 500 race. So, rather than world-class skiers, skaters, and sledders, the audience watched a couple of good ol' boys bump, grind, and duel to the checkered flag in one of stock car racing's most fabulous finishes ever.

For NASCAR, the surprising turn of broadcasting events couldn't have come at a better time. Baseball, football, and basketball had long ruled the sports pages and airwaves nationwide. Stock car racing, meanwhile, was still vying for media attention beyond its local Southern roots. There had been bits and

A TV producer at a NASCAR race has to juggle images being sent from dozens of cameras.

pieces of auto races on TV since the 1960s, but there had never been anything as dramatic as this duel at Daytona. Now, zooming into America's living rooms, came NASCAR's two brightest stars and winningest drivers of that era, David Pearson and Richard Petty. They also just happened to be fierce rivals, along the lines of baseball's Yankees vs. Red Sox or football's Packers vs. Lions. "When David and I hooked up, everyone knew it was going to be exciting," The King—as Petty was affectionately known—once said. "We raced hard."

Well, at least every NASCAR fan knew that, and now millions of newcomers were seeing for themselves what all the excitement was about. It came down to the very last of the race's 200 laps, with Petty's No. 43 Dodge only a couple of inches ahead of Pearson's No. 21 Mercury—both hurtling at a speed somewhere around 150 mph. The capacity crowd of 125,000 racing fans rose to their feet as the white flag dropped, signaling the final go-round. The suspense built as the TV cameras held tight on the daredevil duo of Petty and Pearson.

They approached the steeply banked Turn 3 on the 2.5-mile track. Pearson steered his race car high, close to the outside wall, and swiped the lead, but only for an instant. As The King dove low to the inside of the track to pass his rival, the cars came too close to each other and bumped. The impact sent both into the wall and out of control. Pearson's Mercury spun to a stop near pit road; Petty's Dodge slid onto the grassy infield. The finish line loomed barely 100 feet away—a third of a football field to the checkered flag. Petty, his engine stalled, then watched in helpless agony as Pearson's still-running car crept, at 20 mph, to an incredible victory.

What a wild coming-out party for NASCAR! That thrilling race set the stage for a steady rise in media coverage of the NASCAR Cup Series. The stock car association recognized the opportunity and seized it, granting easy access to its races and colorful drivers, something lacking in other sports. Before long, entire races were being telecast. Within the next 25 years, all 30-plus NASCAR events found a home on TV. In 2001, NASCAR joined sportscasting's big leagues by signing a multi-year contract with NBC and Fox.

Today, every single NASCAR NEXTEL Cup Series race is televised live from start to finish—green flag to checkered flag. So are Friday qualifying runs and Saturday races in the series just below the NASCAR NEXTEL Cup Series. Several cable networks produce regularly scheduled NASCAR-only programs. Major newspapers and magazines send reporters and photographers to every race weekend. The sport is all over the Internet, from NASCAR's own feature-filled web site (read the accompanying story on page 72) to sites set up by individual drivers, by sponsors, by sports media, and by a host of independent entities. (See the list on page 73.)

More than any other source, TV has had the greatest impact on bringing NASCAR to the masses. What makes watching a NASCAR race must-see TV for three-plus hours is how broadcasters present so much more than simply shots of 43 race cars speeding around a track. Broadcasters have cameras everywhere—in the grandstands, on the turns, in the pits and garages, and overhead in helicopters. There are even tiny cameras inside the cars themselves. In addition to the announcers following the action from the main broadcast booth, there are reporters scattered throughout the track.

Just as a driver relies on his entire team to prepare for and run a race, teamwork is the main ingredient in putting that race on the air. NBC Sports, for example, has about 150 people on its NASCAR team, including announcers, reporters, camera

Driver Elliott Sadler takes time to talk to a reporter.

operators, technical engineers, producers, directors, writers, editors, and researchers. Most of them do their work behind the scenes, so viewers rarely see or hear from them.

One of NBC's out-of-sight team members is Sam Flood, the head producer. "I'm like the coach of a football team," he says. "My job is to make sure we have a game plan for each race. I also make sure that everyone on the team works together to win the game. We win the game by putting on a great TV show that tells the story of what happened during that week's race."

Flood begins developing a new game plan almost immediately after the race he's working on wraps up. By Monday morning, he's back in his office in New York City, going over details with various members of the team. Because every track is different, the game plan will be specifically designed to fit that venue.

Meanwhile, as many as eight huge trucks loaded with broadcasting gear are already on their way to the next destination. Throughout the week, researchers and writers will gather news, statistics, and other background information to be used by the announcers. Interviews with drivers, crew chiefs, and NASCAR officials are taped for airing during the race.

The team arrives at the track on Thursday and gets right to work. Dozens of cameras need to be set up (NBC brought 79 to a recent Brickyard 400) in the broadcast booth, at strategic spots around the track, in the pits, and inside 10 race cars. Flood settles into his main control center, a 50-foot tractor-trailer filled with high-tech equipment. There's a wall stacked with TV monitors (one connected to every camera), videotape recorders and players, editing stations, instant-replay machines, and computers for creating the animation and graphics that viewers will see on TV.

Keep in mind that most of the broadcasting equipment has to be wired, with thousands of feet of

This cameraman literally captures a bird's-eye view of the race from high above the track.

TV cameras capture the action of a NASCAR race from dozens of angles and locations.

cable, to a source of electricity. So NBC brings two trucks that are actually huge generators on wheels. Another truck carries transmitters that send live images of the race to a satellite up in space. Moments later, the satellite beams the images to receivers back on Earth, which then send them to millions of TV sets across the country.

When Sunday morning dawns, still several hours before the race goes on the air, the TV crew makes its final plans and preparations. Flood meets with the on-air team, including several pit reporters and the three announcers who will call the race from the main broadcast booth. Flood discusses last-minute details and how to cover the prerace show. The announcers walk through the pits to visit with some of the drivers and their crews.

"We attend the drivers' meeting, and then head up to the booth for rehearsals," says Allen Bestwick, NBC's play-by-play announcer. He's joined by two analysts, Benny Parsons and Wally Dallenbach, both also former NASCAR drivers. (Read the accompanying story on page 70 on Bestwick's race-day duties.)

Once the race starts, the TV team—and the other members of the media—kick into high gear. With Flood in the control truck is director Mike Wells. "I'm wearing a radio headset, talking to the camera operators and telling them what to shoot," Wells says. He's in contact with the pit reporters and coordinating when they go on the air. He also decides what graphics and taped pieces will be shown to viewers. "It's quite a juggling act," says Wells. "We call it 'controlled chaos.'"

At the same time, radio announcers are calling the race from their broadcast booths. Print and web site journalists, sitting at long desks up in the press section, are typing away on their laptops, writing stories that will appear in newspapers, magazines, and online. Other reporters are roaming around the pits and track on the lookout for breaking news.

It was a much smaller and far different media scene at the 1976 Daytona 500, when David Pearson and Richard "The King" Petty introduced NASCAR auto racing to a national audience. But the hundreds of individuals covering today's races can look back fondly on that day as the start of something really big.

Team "spotters" sit high above the track and relay information to the crew chief and driver.

A Day in the Booth

Allen Bestwick goes to work in what he calls "the best seat in the house." He's not kidding. As the play-by-play announcer for NBC Sports' and TNT's coverage of NASCAR NEXTEL Cup Series races, perched high above the track in the broadcast booth, Bestwick can survey all the action. And that's a good thing, because he needs to tell millions of TV viewers exactly what's happening from start to finish. Who's leading? Where's the points leader? Is Tony Stewart setting up to pass Matt Kenseth?

"I take my knowledge of what's going on and deliver it to the people not fortunate to be at the racetrack," Bestwick says. "And I try to do it in an entertaining way."

While Bestwick provides the details, he relies on the color analysts next to him in the booth, Benny Parsons and Wally Dallenbach, to explain why things happen. Why did Stewart make that pass from the inside? Why didn't Dale Jr. make a pit stop when the other leaders did?

Inside the booth, Bestwick sits in front of several TV monitors, so he can see exactly what the viewers at

home are watching. Throughout the week, he makes notes about different drivers on his laptop computer that he can refer to during the broadcast.

The hardest thing about covering a race, he says, is keeping track of 43 cars at the same time. "If you call a football game, there's just one ball to cover, and it's the same with baseball and basketball. But where's the ball in a NASCAR race?"

What a Site to See

NASCAR.com is one of the most fact-, feature-, and fun-filled sports web sites on the Internet. The colorful, jam-packed homepage serves as the gateway to an online bonanza of NASCAR news, race reports and schedules, statistics, driver and crew interviews, historical features, games and contests, photos and video clips, and interactive bonuses.

Clicking on "Drivers" from the menu bar takes visitors to an area containing an A to Z list of biographies of everyone currently in the NASCAR NEXTEL Cup Series, including info on their cars, teams, and sponsors. There's another alphabetical database containing bios on every NASCAR Cup Series driver who has raced in an official NASCAR points event since 1975.

Back on the menu bar, go to "Know Your NASCAR" for a glossary of terms, an explanation of the points system used to determine championships, and stories on women who've competed in NASCAR.

The site's coolest area is TrackPass, although members have to pay a monthly or annual fee to log on. It's packed with an assortment of live, interactive

features that fans can access during a race, such as PitCommand, which follows the pack around the track, timing and scoring, real-time RPMs and speeds, and in-car audio.

Other NASCAR Web Sites

www.msnbc.com—Leads to NBC Sports' and TNT's NASCAR coverage

www.foxsports.com—Ditto for Fox and FX coverage

www.speedtv.com— The companion site to cable's Speed Channel

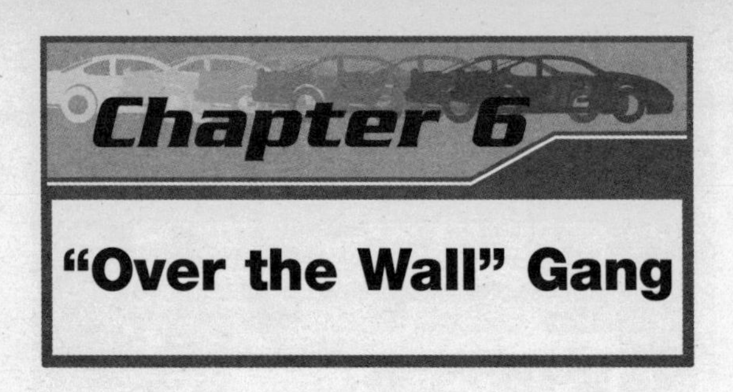

"Over the Wall" Gang

If there's one word that describes what NASCAR is all about, it's "speed." After the racing team is assembled, after the car and engine are built and set up, after the competitors arrive at the track, and after the starter's green flag is dropped, winning the race comes down to speed. Only one car will go faster than the others, pass first under the checkered flag, and stand alone in Victory Lane.

Many factors go into creating speed, some major, others minor. Correcting the shape of the car's body in the shop to make it more aerodynamic is major. Adjusting tire pressure during the middle of a race to compensate for a hot track is minor. One of the biggest and most important elements of speed that contributes to winning in NASCAR is the pit crew. It might seem odd to heap so much credit on seven guys who change tires and gas up the car, but the speed

Kasey Kahne's pit crew awaits his car's arrival on pit road.

with which they perform those duties is absolutely crucial. Any driver will tell you races are won and lost along pit road.

Now imagine this: In the time it took to read the two previous paragraphs in this chapter, a pit stop can be completed. An average efficient pit stop, which consists of changing all four tires and refilling the 22-gallon fuel cell, can take between 13 and 15 seconds! It's easy to see why the slightest mistake can mess up a pit stop — and possibly cost a driver the race.

The members of today's NASCAR pit crews take their jobs very seriously. And it is a real job for many of them. In most cases, they've worked their way up through stock car racing's minor leagues to earn a place on a NASCAR NEXTEL Cup Series team. It's similar to baseball, where a player can spend years coming up through a team's farm system before proving that he's good enough to make it in the major leagues.

These dedicated professionals may have other duties with the team, usually as mechanics, but serving on the pit crew is the most important. They constantly train and practice to improve their times and teamwork. They work out to stay in tip-top shape; lifting 75-pound gas cans and 90-pound tires in a split-second is no easy feat. Pit crews even show off their talents against one another by entering competitions. There's none bigger than the annual World Pit Crew Championships (see accompanying story on page 84).

According to NASCAR rules, in most races, seven members of the pit crew are allowed to go "over the wall" to service the car on pit road. The pit road is the area, usually located along the front straightaway of the track, where the cars are serviced during the race. There is an actual short wall between the pit crews' stations and their pit stalls, the designated spaces where the cars stop. At certain times, NASCAR will allow an eighth member over the wall to clean the windshield. (Think of big, squishy flying bugs going *splat!* at 150 mph!) One of the other crew members behind the wall passes the driver a drink, using a long pole.

The number of pit stops during a NASCAR NEXTEL Cup Series race varies depending on various factors such as:

• The length of a race. For instance, there's more gas consumed during the Daytona 500 than the New England 300. There isn't a fuel gauge in the car, so most teams have a crew member who does nothing but keep track of fuel mileage during a race. It's not

Brian Vickers' car (right) pits as Kevin Harvick's Monte Carlo races back onto the track at the 2004 Pocono 500.

Tide
SUNOCO
GMAC
25
GMAC
25

uncommon for a car to run out of gas near the end of a race, so that's obviously an important job.

• Weather conditions. The hotter the track, the quicker tires wear down. To make it fair for all the drivers, every team uses the same type of special racing tires, made by Goodyear. To help monitor tire conditions, there are "wear pins" inserted in the tires, which become more visible as the tire wears down.

• Caution flags. NASCAR rules mandate cars must stay in order—no passing—while an accident is cleared. That caution period can present an opportunity for a team to pit and avoid having to stop later.

• A team's pit strategy. For example, a decision to change two tires rather than all four can save precious seconds.

The driver and crew chief—whose job typically includes overseeing the pit crew—talk to each other by two-way radio throughout the race, and they decide when it's best to pit. The crew gets the word and prepares to jump into action. They're like sprinters lining up in starting blocks. The driver may need a lap or two to get his car in position to exit the track at the pit entry way, located just before the final turn on most ovals. A crew member holds up a large sign with the driver's car number to show him where to stop.

The moment the car is one pit stall away, the pit crew is over the wall in a flash.

The synchronized septet instantly swarms the car as it comes to a stop. The jack man scrambles to the right side of the car (the side closest to the track). Using a 75-pound, hand-pump jack that rolls underneath the car, he lifts that side of the car completely off the ground in one or two pumps. Simultaneously, the rear tire changer and the front tire changer unscrew the five lug nuts that attach each tire and metal wheel to the axle. They use air-powered impact wrenches, or air guns. (An air gun is attached to a long hose that stretches over the wall to an air compressor, so the crew has to be careful not to trip over it.) Two tire changers grab the old tires and hand the changers new ones, with new lug nuts already glued in place to them. Once the tires are on the car and the lug nuts are screwed on and tightened with the air gun, the jack man lowers the car. Then those five scurry to the left side (the side closest the wall) to repeat the process.

Meanwhile, the gas man is hoisting the first of two 11-gallon gas cans and dumping the gas into the fuel cell. The pipe-shaped neck of the can has a valve at the end that fits snugly into the car's gas port. But in case any gas spills out, the catch-can man holds a

Dale Jarrett's tire changers and jack man do their thing during a pit stop.

special container to the car's overflow vent to catch it. This precaution helps prevent fires from starting. It's also why pit crews are required to wear fireproof suits. After the second can of gas is emptied into the car, the catch-can man raises his hand to signal to the rest of the crew that the refueling process is complete.

Throughout the pit stop, a NASCAR official walks around the car to make sure everything is done by the rules and that safety measures are being followed. Penalties for using the wrong equipment or procedures can cost a driver time or laps. On the other side of the wall are several support crew members who hand tires back and forth to the changers and gas cans to the gas man. And it's all over in less than 20 seconds. The driver's barely had time enough to catch his breath and maybe have a sip of water. Then he hits the gas pedal, and the car rockets back onto the track. At the same time the crew gets ready for the next pit stop. "It's very choreographed," says one crew chief, who stands on a special platform to orchestrate the action. "It can be almost like a ballet. You've got these big tires, running men, and the flying hose of the air gun."

Ballet? Jitterbug might be a better description.

Battle of the Pit Crews

NASCAR NEXTEL Cup Series drivers aren't the only ones who compete every year for a championship. Their pit crews have a chance to be crowned "best of the best," too, at the World Pit Crew Championship. The event has been held annually since 1967 as a chance for the "over-the-wall" guys to shine.

The object of the competition is for each crew in the top 25 in the points standings to empty 14 gallons of gas (two cans holding seven gallons each) into their car's fuel cell and change both left- and right-side tires in as short a time as possible. Time penalties are assessed for various infractions, including loose lug nuts, fuel spills, and fuel left in the gas can. The team with the fastest time becomes the new world champion.

Leonard Wood and his Wood Brothers crew—credited with revolutionizing pit road in the 1960s—were the first champions, appropriately enough, changing two tires in 21.992 seconds. Before the Wood Brothers began assigning specific tasks to crew members, and using three-pump jacks and specialized gas cans, the best pit stops often lasted more than a minute.

In 2003, Bill Elliott's No. 9 Dodge Squad, led by

crew chief Mike Ford, set a new world record of 16.725 seconds. In addition to $30,000 awarded to the pit crew champs, the team received a $10,000 bonus for setting the record.

"I'm just so proud of these guys," said Elliott afterward. "They put in the practice and the effort every day to be the best pit crew, and it makes my job easier. I see how hard these guys work and the amount of pressure they are under. They do a great job."

Here's to the Fans

Getting ready for a NASCAR NEXTEL Cup Series race takes a lot of preparation. All week long, the team spends grueling hours getting the car set up, checking that the gear is in order, loading stuff for the trip, and making sure the rest of the team is primed for race day's high-speed action.

Yes, it's quite a job being a NASCAR fan! It takes planning and teamwork to haul the family to a NASCAR NEXTEL Cup Series race. But considering the many rewards—cheering for your favorite driver, seeing stock car racing's top stars in person, barbecuing hot dogs and hamburgers in the infield, sharing a good ol' time with hundreds of thousands of fellow fans—it's worth every ounce of effort. No wonder nearly seven million loyal NASCAR fans attend the 36 NASCAR NEXTEL Cup Series races every season, which begins in February with the

NASCAR fans are part of the action at a race.

Veteran driver Jeff Gordon gives a fan an autograph.

Daytona 500 and lasts through November's Ford 400 at Homestead-Miami Speedway. Counting the hundreds of other racing series held under the NASCAR banner annually, stock car racing has become the No. 1 spectator sport in America.

In NASCAR's early days, most of the racetracks were located throughout the Southern states where the sport began, so naturally the fans were concentrated in that part of the country, too. But as the NASCAR Cup Series grew and grew, new tracks sprang up far and wide, in states such as Texas, New Hampshire, Pennsylvania, Michigan, California, Delaware, and Arizona. That expansion gradually widened NASCAR fandom to what's now a full-fledged national phenomenon.

To best experience the sights, sounds, smells, and tastes that combine to make attending a live NASCAR event so sensational, there's nothing like the Daytona 500, or the "Great American Race" as the fans have come to know this annual event. It actually encompasses an entire week of celebration. To NASCAR fans, Daytona is the Super Bowl, the World Series, the NBA Finals, and the Stanley Cup Finals rolled into one glorious, star-studded happening. And although it's the first race of the year, rather than the postseason finale, the Daytona 500 has always been *the* race for both drivers and fans.

More than a quarter of a million people descend upon the sunny, sandy shores of Daytona Beach, Florida, every year for the 500. More than any other NASCAR NEXTEL Cup Series race, the full spectrum of the NASCAR fandom is reflected here, from the diehards who return year after year to first-timers who can't resist the lure any longer, from blue-collar workers to Wall Street executives. Men, women, and children; senior citizens and teenagers; individuals and big families; they pack the grandstands, luxury suites, and the infield, which itself becomes a small city during the seven days of Speedweek. Fans arrive in cars, trucks, vans, motorcycles, and RVs (recreational vehicles), as well as private airplanes, jets, and helicopters. The traffic can be pretty jammed-up getting in and out of Daytona International Speedway, especially on race day, but that never keeps the crowds from coming.

There are a handful of sports venues that generate awe at first sight: baseball's Yankee Stadium, football's Lambeau Field, horse racing's Churchill Downs, golf's Augusta National Golf Course, tennis' Center Court at Wimbledon—and Daytona. When it originally opened in 1959, the 2.5-mile, tri-oval superspeedway was a dream-come-true for NASCAR founder Bill France. An auto mechanic with a passion for fast cars, France had moved to Daytona Beach from his native Washington, D.C. in 1934. The hard-packed sand beaches and adjacent Highway A1A were already the scene for stock car races, but Big Bill (he stood 6 feet, 5 inches and weighed 220 pounds) envisioned something grander, a showcase for the emerging sport and its daring drivers.

"There have been other tracks that separated the men from the boys," said driver Jimmy Thompson shortly before the first Daytona 500. "This is the track that will separate the brave from the weak after the boys are gone."

The scene was electric for that inaugural 500, held on February 22, 1959. The 42,000 fans had never seen anything quite like this tremendous track and its four, steeply angled, 31-degree banked turns—about the height of a four-story building from the outside wall down to the infield grass. The banked turns allowed cars to whip around the turns at full speed. Following the glorious opening ceremonies, fans were treated to a thrilling race, which ended with a photo finish between Lee Petty and Johnny Beauchamp. Officials needed two and a half days to review photos and film before determining that Petty had crossed the finish line first—by two feet!

The 480-acre track complex has undergone numerous upgrades over the years. Today, Daytona International Speedway, which includes the interactive Daytona USA entertainment center, is more than a racetrack. It's NASCAR's masterpiece, and fans flock to it like pilgrims to a sacred shrine.

While the Daytona 500 remains like no other event on the NASCAR calendar, it also exemplifies what goes on during every NASCAR NEXTEL Cup Series race. The infield fills up with tents, pop-up campers, and RVs throughout the week. Qualifying and practice runs begin on Friday, and there's usually a NASCAR minor-league race on Saturday. So the fans are sufficiently warmed up for the main event on Sunday.

Prerace "tailgating"—the cooking, eating, music, and partying in the infield and parking lots—is a fun tradition. Fans walk around decked out in caps, T-shirts, and other clothing that display unswerving loyalty to their favorite driver. They line up at souvenir shops to add to their collections. As each driver is introduced over the public address system, his faithful fans roar with cheers, hopes, and wishes that he'll win the day.

You'll find plenty of flags, fans, and fun at a NASCAR event.

Prerace ceremonies at a NASCAR event are an exciting spectacle.

NASCAR draws a patriotic crowd, with the American flag everywhere as evidence. When the National Anthem is sung, it's an emotional moment. Throw in a fly-by of F-16 jets, and the fans are ready. Now it's time for the call, "Gentlemen, start your engines!" A thunderous rumble spreads through the air as the cars pull out from pit road, in the order determined during earlier qualifying laps. The race cars follow the pace car for several warm-up laps. Finally, when the green flag drops—the moment drivers, crews, and fans have been waiting for all week—the race is on. (See chapter 8 for a flag-to-flag description of a NASCAR NEXTEL Cup Series race.)

Many of the rituals before, during, and after a race are fairly common from one track to the next. However, each track has a distinct appeal to fans. A few weeks after Daytona, Darlington—"the track too tough to tame"—delights race fans with its quirky, fender-scraping turns. Then it's on to racing under the lights at cozy Bristol, the short track where the spectators are incredibly close to the action. "There's no other feeling on the circuit like the night race at Bristol," says four-time NASCAR Cup Series champ Jeff Gordon, who has won five races at Bristol. "The drivers get pretty jazzed up about it when we look around and see how cool the atmosphere is there."

The road courses at Infineon and Watkins Glen find fans spreading out to various vantage points around the serpentine tracks' curves, S-turns, and straightaways. Indianapolis Motor Speedway, the hallowed ground of open-wheeled Indy racing (sleeker cars with no fenders), gives way to stock cars for one weekend every summer. Two of the circuit's oldest and grandest tracks, Talladega and Lowe's Motor Speedway, are sprawling facilities. Both are steeped in NASCAR pageantry and lore.

No matter where races are held, fans love NASCAR. "One of the things I like is that every weekend is an all-star race," a hardcore devotee told a reporter for the *Owensboro* (Kentucky) *Messenger-Inquirer* at the 2003 Daytona 500. "Once you go to one race, you're hooked. Just the smell of smoke and burnt rubber, and the energy and people screaming—it's pretty exciting stuff."

See, it is a tough job being a fan...but somebody's got to do it.

There isn't an empty seat to be seen at a NASCAR NEXTEL Cup Series race!

NASCAR Star Gazing

Dale Earnhardt Jr., Matt Kenseth, Jimmie Johnson, Ryan Newman, Jeff Gordon, and other popular NASCAR drivers weren't the only stars that came out for the 2004 Daytona 500. Country-music star LeAnn Rimes got the crowd revved up with a rousing rendition of the National Anthem, Hollywood idol Ben Affleck drove the pace car, and actress Whoopi Goldberg was an honorary starter. Boxer Evander Holyfield, golfer Greg Norman, and other big names

NASCAR fans include actor Ben Affleck and boxer Evander Holyfield.

Country music star Leann Rimes sang the National Anthem at the 2004 Daytona 500.

from the sports world applauded when Miss America Ericka Dunlap sang. But all the jet-setters were overshadowed by the special guest who flew in on Air Force One—President George W. Bush.

Celebrities and politicians are always looking for audiences, and NASCAR has become a major stage. Singers Britney Spears, Sheryl Crow, and Mariah Carey have been spotted at races. Actor John Travolta is an avid fan, and so is actor Keifer Sutherland. Sutherland is such a NASCAR fan he was chosen to be the narrator of the NASCAR IMAX movie.

Chapter 8

A Sunday at the Races

The power of 34,000 horses. More than 146,000 pounds of steel, rubber, and essential fluids. Nearly 950 gallons of gasoline. Forty-three engines, each creating 130 decibels of noise at full throttle—that's almost as much noise as the space shuttle generates when it blasts off! Plus about 185,000 screaming fans. Add it all up, and the start of a NASCAR NEXTEL Cup Series race is an amazing spectacle of sights, sounds, and fast-paced action.

When the NASCAR official, perched high above the starting line, unfurls the green flag to signal the booming, pedal-to-the-metal blastoff for the squadron of 43 race cars, it's a mind-boggling, ear-splitting, eye-popping event. It is also the coming together of time, energy, teamwork, talent, knowledge, experience, money, materials, hopes, and dreams of thousands of dedicated individuals. There's the driver who started

A pace car leads the race cars around the track for several laps just before the actual race starts.

out racing go-carts when he was five and the engine mechanic who studied nights and weekends to earn a college engineering degree. There's the team owner who spent years lining up sponsors, and the fan who drove all night to get to the track on time. Combine all these elements and NASCAR represents the ultimate in human endeavor and accomplishment. It's a whole lot of fun, to boot!

If everyone's lucky, the sun will be shining bright and early on this summery Sunday morning. The temperatures are predicted to rise into the low 80s, with comfortable humidity and scattered puffy white clouds to accent a bright blue sky. The track workers are arriving, getting ready to open the concessions and souvenir shops. Crews are checking the track itself to ensure that it's clear of debris after Saturday night's "happy hour," the time set aside for final practice runs. Fans camped around the infield are awakening, and soon the smells of coffee, bacon, and eggs are wafting through the air. The parking lots await the parade of traffic that's already building on the highways approaching the racetrack.

In the garage area, the racing teams' crews have been busy since dawn, making last-minute adjustments to their cars' engines, setups, and safety equipment. NASCAR inspectors will soon begin their final rounds to ensure everyone's following the rules. The crew chiefs and drivers, after walking the track to check conditions, will go over their strategy for the race one more time. Earlier, the pit crews picked up sets of tires from the central storage area. They're now stacking them and moving gas cans, jacks, air guns, and tools into place just inside the wall they'll be hurtling over in a few hours.

The television crews are bustling, too, firing up the generator trucks and running final tests on cameras and microphones. Producers and directors review the broadcast game plan in the control center truck. The on-air teams and various reporters wander through the garage area, hobnobbing with anyone willing to talk or listen.

The prerace buzz builds throughout the morning. By noon, only an hour before the green flag drops, almost everything and everyone are in place. The official drivers' meeting is over and the cars have been pushed onto pit road. The pit crews are assembled in their safety gear, the grandstands are nearly full, and the radio and TV coverage has begun. In millions of homes across the country, Americans are wrapping up their Sunday-morning activities and chores, getting the snacks, cold beverages, and big-screen TVs ready.

A few minutes after 1 P.M., the 43 gentlemen have started their engines and are on the last of their pace laps. A total of 172 Goodyear tires are softening up and getting a grip on the warming asphalt. Drivers and crew chiefs chat on their two-way radios about how their cars feel. Fans predict “my guy” will beat “your guy.” Then the green flag is waved.

And they’re off! The explosion of engines and cheers is deafening as the cars rocket to triple-digit speeds and begin jockeying and jostling for position. The race might ultimately come down to the final lap, but every single lap counts, so there’s no holding back.

Here’s a hypothetical race: let’s say it’s a 500-miler on a 1.5-mile oval track. That’s 334 laps and a running time, depending on the unpredictable caution flags, of about three-and-a-half-hours. Speeds will average around 135 mph.

Inside the car, the driver is totally focused. Over the first fifty laps or so, he’s responding to his crew chief’s questions about the car’s setup, letting him know if it’s running too loose (not stable enough on the track) or too tight (difficult to steer). How’s the engine sound? Are the gauge readings okay?

In the TV control center, the director cues the

Casey Mears (41), Ricky Rudd (21), Johnny Sauter (30), and Tony Stewart (20) battle for the lead.

camera operators, telling them what to shoot. He's sitting in front of a row of buttons that control which camera goes live. "Ready 10, take 10," he says into his headset. That tells the person operating camera 10, situated at Turn 3, she's on the air. A few seconds later, it's, "Ready 28, take 28." And so on.

Up in the booth, the play-by-play announcer helps viewers follow the action. The running-order ticker continuously updates who's where on the track. It identifies the driver in each place, the number, make, and speed of his car, and how many seconds he is behind the leader. Another graphic follows one or two cars, by number, around the track. Occasionally, an image pops up that looks like a speedometer (though there are none in NASCAR race cars) and tachometer. They show the speed and RPM readings for a particular car in real-time.

Halfway through the race, a pack of 15 cars is following the leader. They're drafting one another around Turn 3, when one car moves high and attempts to make a pass. Instead, he brushes the wall, and the grandstand crowd suddenly rises to its feet. Many of the fans are wearing headphones and listening to the radio announcer while watching what turns out to be a five-car crash. Crashes add an element of excitement to races—as long as no one is seriously hurt.

The yellow caution flag immediately comes out, so every car must instantly slow down and remain in the exact order they were in when the flag was waved. Activity picks up along pit road, because cautions can be a smart time to pit without losing your spot on the track. As the cars start coming in and the frenzy begins, pit reporters describe the scene to viewers. Back in the booth, a color analyst is going over slow-motion replays of the crash—seen from several angles, including an in-car camera—and explaining just what went wrong.

Remember, there's no air-conditioning in these stock cars, so the temperatures in them can climb to well over 100 degrees, even in good weather conditions. The drivers can't even take their hands off the wheel to reach for a bottle of water, so they tough it out until the next pit stop.

This caution lasts for six laps before full-bore racing resumes. In all, there will be seven cautions this Sunday. While there were no stoppages and no one hurt, a half-dozen race cars sustain enough damage to knock them out of the race. There are 24 lead changes among 12 different cars. With 32 laps remaining, three drivers are in contention—one's a rookie, the others are seasoned veterans. On lap 310, one veteran's car slows, and engine trouble ends his afternoon. Now it's down to two.

Fans of the pair are going crazy in the stands. Besides more than $1 million, the winner picks up valuable points. The media's attention is now focused on just two cars. Each car's crew chief has separately calculated that his car has enough fuel to finish without pitting.

The white flag drops indicating one lap to go. The fans zero in on another neck-and-neck duel. As the cars round Turn 4, the rookie challenger tries one last pass, but the savvy leader blocks his way. He takes the checkered flag by less than a car length.

His pit crew breaks into wild celebration during the victory lap, then high-fives the driver when he pops out of the car. A pit reporter is interviewing the crew chief as the car is rolled into Victory Lane, where the postrace partying and analysis begin.

Driver Jimmie Johnson, left and crew chief Chad Knaus hoist the Pocono 500 trophy into the air in Victory Lane.

Just Rewards

Prize money and points are certainly welcome rewards for winning a NASCAR NEXTEL Cup Series race, but victors also win a variety of trophies and awards for their high-speed accomplishments. The NASCAR NEXTEL Cup Series championship trophy, for example, is perhaps the biggest prize given annually to a driver. The winner is the driver who accumulates the most points during a season.

One of the most coveted statuettes, though, is the Harley J. Earl Trophy, given to the winner of the Daytona 500. It seems that Earl, the legendary car designer for General Motors from the 1930s to the 1960s (best known for the Corvette), was a racing fan and friend of NASCAR founder Bill France. France demonstrated his friendship and respect for Earl by naming the trophy after him.

Here are some other unique driver awards and rewards:

• Trophies at Tennessee's Nashville Superspeedway, located in the capital of country music, are actually specially designed Gibson Les Paul guitars.

• A grandfather clock has been the traditional trophy for winners at Virginia's Martinsville Speedway since the mid-1960s.

• At the Brickyard 400, held at the Indianapolis Motor Speedway, the highest-qualifying rookie and his crew chief have their names engraved on the Golden Walrus trophy, which is put on display at the track's museum.

• Ryan Newman was honored as the 2003 Speed Channel Driver of the Year during the International Motorsports Hall of Fame's annual induction ceremonies with the presentation of a trophy and a Victory motorcycle.

Ryan Newman

PHOTOGRAPHY CREDITS

Title page, pages 11, 17, 19, 24, 26, 27, 34, 39, 48, 50, 51, 52, 53, 54, 55, 57, 59, 63, 65, 66, 69, 78, 82, 85, 87, 88, 97, 98, 99, 101, 105, 109, 111, all cover images.
Sherryl Creekmore/NASCAR

pages 29, 31, 75, 93, 94
CIA Stock Photography, Inc.

page 56
Action Sports Photography, Inc.

page 7
Steven Rose/MMP, Inc.